Chhath Puja

AF657577

Contributors: Sujata Saha

Purwa Chakraborty

Publisher: Divinebharat

ISBN: 978-93-5627-980-3

Contributors: Sujata Saha
Purwa Chakraborty
Publisher: Divinebharat

For permissions, bulk orders, or any other information, please contact:
info.divinebharat@gmail.com
www.divinebharat.co

Table of Contents

Introduction

Chhath Mahaparv is an ancient folk vow and folk festival associated with the worship of **Surya Dev** (the Sun God) and **Chhathi Maiya**. It is rooted in the tradition of expressing gratitude toward nature, water, and the sun. This festival is traditionally celebrated mainly in the Indian states of Bihar, Jharkhand, eastern Uttar Pradesh, and West Bengal, as well as in the Madhesh/Terai regions of Nepal. Over time, Indian and Nepali diaspora communities have also begun celebrating this festival in many countries around the world.
The distinctive feature of Chhath Puja lies in its simplicity, strict discipline, and collective nature. Offerings (arghya) are made to the sun at sunset and sunrise, and only natural and pure materials are used in the worship.

Chhath Puja is observed twice a year—

- **Chaiti Chhath:** In the month of Chaitra according to the Vikram Samvat
- **Kartik Chhath:** In the month of Kartik according to the Vikram Samvat (the main and most widely observed Chhath)

During this festival, Surya Dev and Chhathi Maiya (Chhathi Mata) are worshipped with prayers for the well-being of children, family prosperity, and overall auspiciousness in life. Surya Dev is revered as the source of life on earth and is offered prayers for blessings and the fulfillment of personal wishes. Chhathi Maiya is regarded as the sixth form of nature, the sister of Surya Dev, and a goddess born from the sixth element of creation. In scriptures and folk traditions, she is considered the protector of children and a deity associated with family welfare. It is believed that the worship of Chhathi Maiya must be performed with discipline, purity, and prescribed rituals, and that this vow may be observed equally by both women and men. The worship of Chhathi Maiya is deeply connected with folk faith, tradition, and nature worship, which together form the foundation of this festival.

Chhath Puja is also known by several names—**Chhait, Chhath Parv, Chhath Puja, Dala Chhath, Dal Puja, and Surya Shashthi.**

This festival is mainly observed by Indian and Nepali communities. Prominent linguistic and cultural groups associated with Chhath Puja include the Bhojpuri, Magahi, Maithili, and Tharu communities.The main observer of the Chhath vow is called a **Parvaitin**, a term derived from the Sanskrit word *"Parva"*. Parvaitins are generally women, though men also observe this vow. The fast is undertaken for the welfare of the family and the well-being of children.

Chhath Puja does not require a temple or an idol. The worship is performed near rivers, ponds, or other clean water sources. Bamboo baskets and winnowing trays (soop) are used for offering arghya. Prasad and puja items are prepared using clay, bamboo, and other natural materials. Devotees often walk barefoot to the ghat. The presence of a priest is not mandatory, as families and communities collectively participate in the rituals. All devotees follow the same procedure and offer identical prasad. During Chhath Puja, no distinction is made based on caste, class, or social status.

Chhath Puja is observed over four days. It begins on Kartik Shukla Chaturthi and concludes on Kartik Shukla Saptami. The Chhath vow is considered one of the most rigorous fasts.
The rituals are completed through four prescribed observances—
Nahay-Khay, Kharna (Lohanda), Evening Arghya, and Morning Arghya.
The festival concludes after the offering of the morning arghya.

This book has been prepared to help devotees perform Chhath Puja in a traditional and systematic manner, presenting the essential rituals, mantras, and observances in an orderly sequence.

Chhath Puja Materials List

1. Ganga Water / Pure Water
    - Milk
    - Honey
2. Lamps and Worship Items
    - Earthen lamps (clay diyas)
    - Oil
    - Cotton wicks
    - Dhoop sticks
    - Incense sticks
    - Camphor
    - Sandalwood (chandan)
    - Kumkum
    - Roli / Sindoor
    - Flowers
    - Flower garlands
3. Grains and Prasad Items
    - Arwa rice (raw rice)
    - Wheat flour
    - Jaggery
    - Thekua
    - Khaja
    - Gujiya
    - Laddoos

- Makhana (fox nuts)
- Rice laddoos / Kachwaniya

4. Fruits and Root Vegetables
   - Banana
   - Large lemon
   - Coconut (with water)
   - Sugarcane
   - Custard apple (Sharifa)
   - Pear
   - Water chestnut (Singhara)
   - Sweet potato (Suthni)
   - Radish
   - Brinjal (eggplant)
   - Pumpkin

5. Vessels and Utensils
   - Bamboo winnowing tray (Soop)
   - Bamboo basket (Dala)
   - Brass / copper lota (water pot)
   - Kalash
   - Plate (thali)
   - Earthen vessels

6. Other Essential Items
   - Betel leaves
   - Areca nut (supari)

- Sacred thread (kalava)
- Turmeric
- Ginger (green plant)
- Sugarcane sticks with 5 or 7 leaves

7. New Clothes (for the observer)
    - Gamcha

Traditional Prasad of Chhath Puja

1. **Thekua:** Prepared from wheat flour, jaggery, and ghee. The main and indispensable prasad of Chhath Puja
2. **Kheer:** Kheer made from milk and jaggery. Especially offered on the day of Kharna
3. Fruits and Other Prasad

•Banana
•Sugarcane
•Large lemon (Dabh)
•Coconut
•Custard apple (Sharifa)
•Water chestnut (Singhara)
•Sweet potato (Suthni)
•Pumpkin
•Seasonal fruits

Rules to Be Observed During Chhath Puja (Day-wise)

First Day — Nahay-Khay
(Kartik Shukla Chaturthi)

The first day of Chhath Puja is known as **Nahay-Khay**. From this day, the Chhath vow formally begins, and the observer starts practicing purity, restraint, and discipline. On this day, devotees bathe before sunrise in a sacred river such as the Ganga. Where a river is not accessible, bathing is done at home by mixing Ganga water with regular water. After bathing, clean clothes are worn and the vow of Chhath is solemnly undertaken.

Following this, the entire house is thoroughly cleaned, and all items to be used for the puja are purified. From the day of Nahay-Khay onward, special care is taken to maintain purity, simplicity, and sattvic conduct within the household.

Only sattvic food is consumed on this day, and the use of garlic, onion, and regular salt is strictly prohibited. The main meal consists of pumpkin (lauki), chana dal, and arwa rice. Foods prepared with jaggery and mustard greens are considered especially auspicious. This food is prepared in new utensils, using a stove or gas, following strict cleanliness. Along with the fasting observer, all family members partake in the same meal.

On the day of Nahay-Khay, food is eaten only once. Before the meal, an offering is made to Surya Dev, after which the food is consumed while sitting on the ground. Charity and acts of merit hold special significance on this day. According to one's capacity, donating rice, milk, or yellow clothes to the poor or needy is considered auspicious.

Thus, the day of Nahay-Khay lays the foundation of complete physical, mental, and household purity for the observance of the Chhath vow.

Second Day — Kharna / Lohanda

(Kartik Shukla Panchami)

The second day of Chhath Puja is known as **Kharna**, observed on the Panchami tithi of the Shukla Paksha in the month of Kartik. On this day, the fasting observer observes a complete **nirjala fast** (without food or water) throughout the day and partakes in food only after sunset. The Kharna vrat is generally observed at home, where the worship and preparation of prasad take place in a clean and peaceful environment. Visiting a river or ghat is not required on this day.

On the day of Kharna, prasad such as **kheer made from jaggery**, **wheat flour rotis**, **thekua**, and fruits (such as banana and custard apple) are prepared. Special care is taken to ensure complete purity and sanctity of the prasad. Fruits and flowers must not be cut or tasted beforehand, the prasad must be kept away from birds, and touching it with unclean hands is strictly prohibited. The prasad is cooked on a **clay stove** using **mango wood**, in **earthen or brass**

utensils. Gas or modern cooking methods are not used. The prasad is prepared exclusively by the fasting observer, maintaining complete ritual purity. Throughout the entire vow period, cleanliness, restraint, and disciplined conduct are strictly observed.

After sunset, the observer bathes and wears clean clothes. Thereafter, meditating upon **Surya Dev** and **Chhathi Maiya**, the prasad is offered as bhog and an aarti is performed. After the offering, the fasting observer partakes of the prasad first, followed by the other family members. With the consumption of the Kharna prasad, a **continuous 36-hour rigorous nirjala fast** begins. This fast continues until the offering of the evening arghya on the following day and concludes after offering arghya to the rising sun. During this period, the observer leads a simple life and sleeps on a mat laid on the ground instead of a bed. Thus, Kharna is considered a sacred symbolizing self-discipline, purity, and unwavering devotion.

Third Day — Evening Arghya

(Kartik Shukla Shashthi)

The third day of Chhath Puja is known as **Evening Arghya**, and it is regarded as the most important and central day of Chhath Mahaparv. This observance takes place on the Shashthi tithi of the Shukla Paksha in the month of Kartik. On this day, the fasting observer continues a strict **nirjala fast** throughout the day and night. The consumption of food and water is completely prohibited.

In the morning, the observer bathes and wears clean clothes, maintaining restraint, silence, purity, and devotion throughout the day. Preparations for the Chhath Puja prasad are carried out at home. All items are prepared with complete cleanliness and care, avoiding any form of impurity.

Preparation of Prasad and Soop (Dala)

For the Evening Arghya, the prasad includes thekua, sugarcane, bananas, coconut, water chestnut, apples or other seasonal fruits, rice laddoos, lemons, and similar offerings. All these items are arranged in bamboo soops, dalas, or baskets. Bamboo is considered a symbol of natural purity and sattvic quality; therefore, metal or plastic containers are not used.

The soop/dala generally contains:

- Thekua
- Whole coconut
- Sugarcane
- Bananas and other fruits
- Rice laddoos
- Lamp (earthen diya)
- Lota with pure water and milk

Proceeding to the Ghat

Before sunset, the observer proceeds with family members toward a river, pond, reservoir, or ghat. Family members carry the soops and other offerings on their heads or in their hands with reverence. This journey is filled with devotion and festive joy.

Method of Offering Arghya

Upon reaching the ghat, the observer faces the west and, in many places, stands in water up to the waist. Holding the bamboo soop or dala, the prasad is raised toward the sun, and arghya is offered to the setting sun.

Arghya is offered using:

- Pure water and milk
- Prasad

Prayers and Sentiments During Arghya

At this time, the observer reverently remembers Surya Dev and Chhathi Maiya. In many regions, prayers are offered with sentiments such as:

"He Surya Dev, He Chhathi Maiya, Hamari shraddha swikar karen, Santan, swasthya aur sukh-samriddhi pradan karen."

In several places, folk songs dedicated to Chhathi Maiya are sung according to local tradition. These songs express devotion, compassion, and prayers for family welfare. Generally, no aarti is performed at this time; the worship is completed through arghya and folk songs.

Role of the Family

Family members remain present at the ghat along with the observer, helping manage the prasad, lighting lamps, and participating in the worship with full devotion. This collective worship symbolizes family unity and shared values.

Kosi (Lighting of Lamps)

After the Evening Arghya, the ritual of **Kosi** is performed, usually in the courtyard of the house or another clean place. Five or seven lamps are arranged in earthen vessels and lit using ghee or mustard oil. These lamps are offered to Chhathi Maiya along with sugarcane, fruits, and thekua. During the Kosi ritual, the observer prays for peace in the home, well-being of children, and prosperity.

Night-time Discipline

After Kosi, the Chhath Vrat Katha is recited. In many places, there is also a tradition of staying awake through the night. Throughout the night, the observer maintains restraint and purity and sleeps on a mat laid on the ground.

Continuation of the Vow

Chhath Puja does not conclude with the Evening Arghya. The vow is completed only after offering arghya to the rising sun (**Morning Arghya**) on the Saptami tithi. The same soops and dalas used on the Shashthi day are used again the next morning.

Thus, the Evening Arghya and its associated rituals stand as sacred symbols of gratitude toward nature, balance in life, family unity, and unwavering devotion.

Fourth Day — Usha Arghya

(Kartik Shukla Saptami)

The fourth and final day of Chhath Puja is known as **Usha Arghya**. It is observed on the Saptami tithi of the Shukla Paksha in the month of Kartik, and on this day the four-day Chhath Mahaparv is formally concluded. This day is regarded as a symbol of new beginnings, renewed energy, gratitude, and the successful completion of the sacred vow.

Tradition of Staying at the Ghat Overnight

Traditionally, in many regions, after the Evening Arghya (on Shashthi tithi), the fasting observers spend the night at the ghat or riverbank itself. After offering arghya and performing the Kosi ritual, the observers remain there for night-long vigil, devotional singing, and remembrance of Chhathi Maiya. This night is considered a symbol of continuous austerity and complete surrender. In some places, the observers sleep on a mat laid on the ground at the ghat and offer the Usha

Arghya from the same place at dawn. During this time, the strict observance of the nirjala fast, silence, and ritual purity is maintained.However, this practice is not mandatory everywhere. In many regions, the observers return home after the Evening Arghya and Kosi, observe night-long vigil at home, and then return to the ghat in the morning to offer Usha Arghya. Both traditions are accepted and respected.

Preparations at Brahma Muhurta

On this day, the observers wake up during **Brahma Muhurta**, bathe, and observe complete ritual purity. The observers and their family members prepare the same soops and dalas with the puja items that were used for the Evening Arghya. Maintaining the sanctity and wholeness of the prasad is considered extremely important.

Proceeding to the Ghat

Before sunrise, the observers proceed with their family members toward the river, pond, reservoir, or ghat. Upon reaching the ghat, the observers stand in the water facing the east and wait for the first rays of the rising sun. Family members manage the soops, prasad, and lamps and participate in the worship with reverence.

Method of Offering Usha Arghya

As soon as the first rays of the sun appear, the observers offer the final arghya to the rising Surya Dev using pure water and milk. At this time, prayers are offered to Surya Dev and Chhathi Maiya for family happiness, prosperity, good health, and long life of children.

After the arghya, in many places the observers circumambulate the ghat **7 or 11 times**. During this, folk songs dedicated to Chhathi Maiya are sung according to local tradition, expressing gratitude, joy, and devotion.

Breaking the Fast (Paran)

The rigorous **36-hour nirjala fast** is broken only after the Usha Arghya. After returning from the ghat, or at the ghat itself, the observer gradually breaks the fast by:

- First consuming plain water, Ganga water, or raw milk
- Then partaking of the prasad offered to Chhathi Maiya, especially thekua and fruits

With this, the vow is formally completed. Only after the observer partakes of the prasad do other family members consume the prasad or food.

Distribution of Prasad and Blessings

After the completion of the vow, the prasad is distributed among family members, neighbors, and present devotees. The observer seeks blessings by touching the feet of elders, while others receive blessings from the observer.

Rules After Paran

Even after breaking the fast, on the same day:

- Only sattvic food is prepared and consumed at home
- Garlic, onion, and tamasic foods remain strictly prohibited
- Restraint, purity, and disciplined conduct are maintained

Significance of Usha Arghya

Usha Arghya is a sacred occasion to express gratitude to Surya Dev. Just as the setting sun is honored during the Evening Arghya, Usha Arghya embodies the spirit of new energy, hope, and the renewal of life. When the fast is broken according to the prescribed method, the observer receives the full spiritual merit of the austerity, and the body gradually returns to its normal state.

Thus, with the offering of Usha Arghya, the four-day sacred observance of Chhath Puja is successfully completed with devotion, discipline, nature worship, and prayers for family well-being.

Chhath Puja Mantras

1. Sankalp Mantra

Om adya (amuk) gotroham (amuk) namaham
Mama sarvapapakshayapurvak
Sharirarogya samriddhi santan sukhapraptyartham
Shri Suryanarayan dev prasannartham
Shri Surya Shashthi vratam karishye

2. Surya Arghya Mantra (Main)

Om aihi Suryadev sahasransho tejorashe jagatpate
Anukampaya mam bhaktya grihanarghya divakarah

3. Surya Arghya Mantra (Optional / Extended)

Om Suryaya namah
Om Adityaya namah
Om namo Bhaskaraya namah
Arghyam samarpayami

4. Suryadev Stuti Mantra
Adideva namastubhyam prasid mam Bhaskar
Divakar namastubhyam Prabhakar namostute

5. Vedic Surya Mantra
Om ghrinim Surya Adityah

6. Beej Mantra (For Japa)
Om hrim hrim Suryaya sahasrakiranaya
Manovanchhit phalam dehi dehi swaha

7. Short Japa During Arghya
Om Suryaya namah

8. Chhathi Maiya Smaran Mantra
Om Chhathi Maiyai namah

9. Smaran Before Breaking the Fast (Paran)
Om namah Suryanarayanaya
Om namah Chhathi Maiyai

Chhath Puja Vrat Katha

Praacheen kaal mein Priyavrat naam ke ek dharmatma raja the. Unki patni ka naam Malini tha. Raja aur rani ke paas dhan vaibhav aur aishwarya ki koi kami nahi thi, parantu ve santanheen the. Santan ki prapti ke liye unhone Maharshi Kashyap se paramarsh liya. Maharshi Kashyap ke nirdesh par raja ne putreshti yagya karaya. Yagya ke prabhav se rani Malini garbhvati hui, kintu durbhagyavash unhonne ek mrit shishu ko janm diya.

Putra viyog se vyathit hokar raja Priyavrat atyant dukhi ho gaye aur shmashan ki or prasthan kiya. Usi samay aakash se ek divya devi prakat hui. Unhone kaha
Rajan main Shashthi Devi hoon. Main prakriti ka chhatha ansh hoon aur samast balakon ki rakshika

hoon. Jo stri purush shraddha aur niyam purvak meri upasana karte hain, unhe santan sukh aur kalyan ki prapti hoti hai.

Devi ke nirdeshanusar raja Priyavrat aur rani Malini ne Kartik maas ke Shukla paksh ki Shashthi tithi ko vidhipurvak Suryadev aur Shashthi Mata ka vrat kiya. Devi ki kripa se unka mrit putra jeevit ho utha. Usi din se Shashthi Mata aur Suryadev ki upasana ka yah vrat prachalit hua, jo aage chalkar Chhath Puja ke naam se jaana gaya.

Ek anya manyata ke anusar Mahabharat kaal mein Pandavon aur Draupadi ne apne vanvaas ke samay yah vrat kiya tha. Suryadev ki kripa se unhe rajya aur samman ki punah prapti hui. Karn jo Suryadev ke putra the, pratidin jal mein khade hokar surya ko arghya dete the. Isi parampara se arghya dene ki vidhi prachalit hui.

Ramayan kaal mein Bhagwan Shri Ram aur Mata Sita ne Ayodhya lautne ke baad Kartik Shukla Shashthi ko Suryadev ki upasana ki. Mata Sita ne yah vrat kiya aur Suryadev ki kripa se unhe santan sukh prapt hua.

Is prakar Chhath Puja Suryadev aur Shashthi Mata ki upasana ka vrat hai, jo niyam shuddhata aur parampara ke saath kiya jata hai.

Chhathi Maiya sabka kalyan kare.

9 789356 279803

Printed at Repro India Ltd.